CELEBRATING THE FAMILY NAME OF LIU

Celebrating the Family Name of Liu

Walter the Educator

Silent King Books
a WhichHead Entertainment Imprint

Copyright © 2024 by Walter the Educator

All rights reserved. No part of this book may be reproduced in any manner whatsoever without written permission except in the case of brief quotations embodied in critical articles and reviews.

First Printing, 2024

Disclaimer

This book is a literary work; the story is not about specific persons, locations, situations, and/or circumstances unless mentioned in a historical context. Any resemblance to real persons, locations, situations, and/or circumstances is coincidental. This book is for entertainment and informational purposes only. The author and publisher offer this information without warranties expressed or implied. No matter the grounds, neither the author nor the publisher will be accountable for any losses, injuries, or other damages caused by the reader's use of this book. The use of this book acknowledges an understanding and acceptance of this disclaimer.

Celebrating the Family Name of Liu is a memory book that belongs to the Celebrating Family Name Book Series by Walter the Educator. Collect them all and more books at WaltertheEducator.com

USE THE EXTRA SPACE TO DOCUMENT YOUR FAMILY MEMORIES THROUGHOUT THE YEARS

LIU

Through misty hills and rivers wide,

The name of Liu flows like the tide.

A beacon bright, a timeless flame,

A legacy built on honor's name.

With every stroke of calligraphic art,

The Liu name beats in history's heart.

From ancient halls to future days,

Their journey weaves through countless ways.

Scholars and sages, poets and seers,

The Liu name whispers across the years.

A lineage vast, a story deep,

Of dreams awakened and vows to keep.

In orchards sweet and bamboo groves,

The Liu name thrives, it always grows.

A family rooted in earth and sky,

Their aspirations reaching high.

With steady hands, they shape the land,

Through wisdom's touch and virtue's stand.

Builders of bridges, both near and far,

The Liu name shines like the evening star.

Through storms they've sailed, through calm they've stayed,

In life's great tapestry, their thread is laid.

A legacy strong, a steadfast hue,

The Liu name rises, proud and true.

In fields of green, in twilight's glow,

The Liu name whispers where winds blow.

A song of peace, of hope, of grace,

A name that holds a sacred space.

From quiet strength to bold command,

The Liu name stands across the land.

Its presence felt in hearts and mind,

A testament to what they find.

Through every dawn, through every night,

The Liu name burns with guiding light.

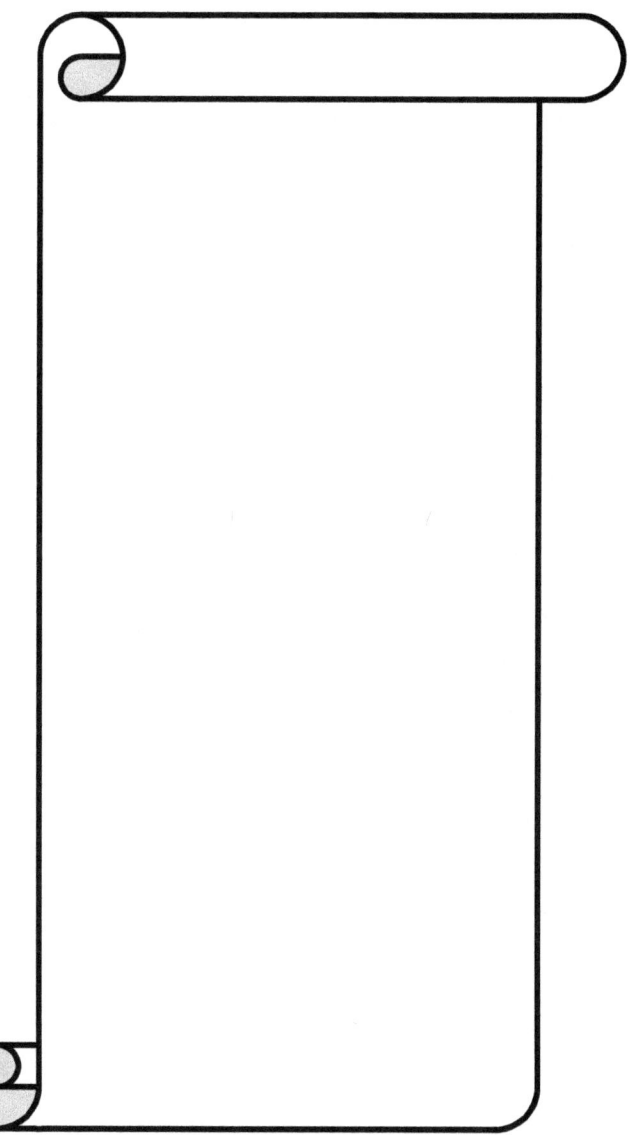

A family's spirit, fierce and free,

An emblem of eternity.

So sing, oh world, of Liu's great name,

A story written in history's frame.

With pride they walk, with honor lead,

A family bound by word and deed.

ABOUT THE CREATOR

Walter the Educator is one of the pseudonyms for Walter Anderson. Formally educated in Chemistry, Business, and Education, he is an educator, an author, a diverse entrepreneur, and he is the son of a disabled war veteran. "Walter the Educator" shares his time between educating and creating. He holds interests and owns several creative projects that entertain, enlighten, enhance, and educate, hoping to inspire and motivate you. Follow, find new works, and stay up to date with Walter the Educator™

at WaltertheEducator.com

www.ingramcontent.com/pod-product-compliance
Lightning Source LLC
LaVergne TN
LVHW012051070526
838201LV00082B/3916